the
coloured pencil
Swatch Book

Just Swatches Edition!

Lila Lilyat
www.KindaKookie.com

Colour
Swatches

medium being swatched
e.g. 'Artsta pencils'

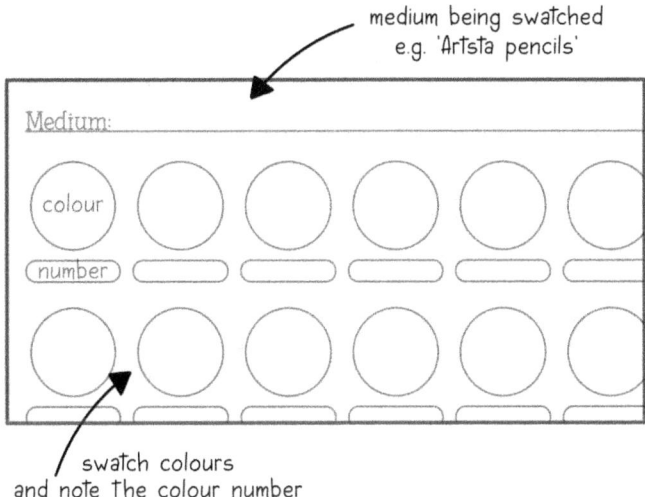

Medium:

colour

number

swatch colours
and note the colour number

Medium: _____

Medium:

Medium:

Medium:

Medium:

Medium:

Medium: _____

Medium:

Medium: _____

Medium:

Medium: _____

Medium:_____

Medium: _____

Medium: _____